WONDERFUL
mini WAFFLES

Deliciously creative recipes taking mini to mighty!

WONDERFUL
mini WAFFLES

by Catherine-Gail Reinhard
and the Editors at Dash

ISBN: 978-0-9971012-5-6

First paperback edition September 2019.
Designed in New York City.
Printed in China.
10 9 8 7 6

Distributed by StoreBound
50 Broad Street, New York, NY 10004
Bydash.com

Full credits & acknowledgements on pg 162
Pictured on the Front Cover: Waffle Pops, pg 132
Pictured on the Back Cover: Dash Mini Waffle Maker

Nobody does it batter!

This book is dedicated to all the
waffle enthusiasts in the world, from
late-night dessert waffle connoisseurs
to early-morning breakfast crusaders.

We love you a waffle lot!

Classic Waffles, pg 14

HELLO!

In this Wonderful Mini Waffles Cookbook, you'll find over 75 new, kitchen-ready waffle recipes. This book includes everything you need to get started making whimsical mini waffle creations at home: From sweet classics to innovative savory treats and everything in between, this cookbook is your guide to making the most of your Dash Mini Waffle Maker.

We've used the common measuring tools (spoons & cups) in writing this book to make it accessible to as many people as possible. We believe that cooking should be fun and mini waffles are a perfect medium to experiment with your creativity in the kitchen, so throw on your apron and jump in!

HAPPY ^ mini WAFFLING!

CONTENTS

WAFFLE
BASICS

THE MINI HISTORY OF WAFFLES

Since introducing our Dash Mini Makers in 2015, we've sold millions of these mighty little appliances. But before you can master the art of mini waffles, let's take a walk through the pages of waffle history...

Waffles first found their way to the USA in the early stages of the 1600s. Dutch settlers brought the recipe to American shores from the Netherlands in the 1620s. In 1906, the first electric waffle iron was invented in Boston. By the 1920s, the waffle iron was a mainstream kitchen appliance. Since then, waffles have been a staple of the classic American breakfast.

Enter the Dash Mini Waffle Maker. The revolutionary product was small in size but massive in impact. Its four-inch dual non-stick cooking surfaces took the world by storm, heating quickly and evenly for delicious results every time. With fans from coast to coast, this mini yet mighty kitchen appliance demands an extensive repertoire of recipes, and thus, *Wonderful Mini Waffles* is poised to change the waffle game once again!

SHORT CUTS

Looking for a way to free yourself from making batter over and over again? We recommend using Aunt Jemima® Original Complete Pancake & Waffle Mix, which only calls for adding water. For the gluten-free crowd, take a look at Bob's Red Mill® Gluten Free Mix and Pamela's® Whole Grain Baking Mix.

WHERE DO I START?

All waffles are made with these simple ingredients:

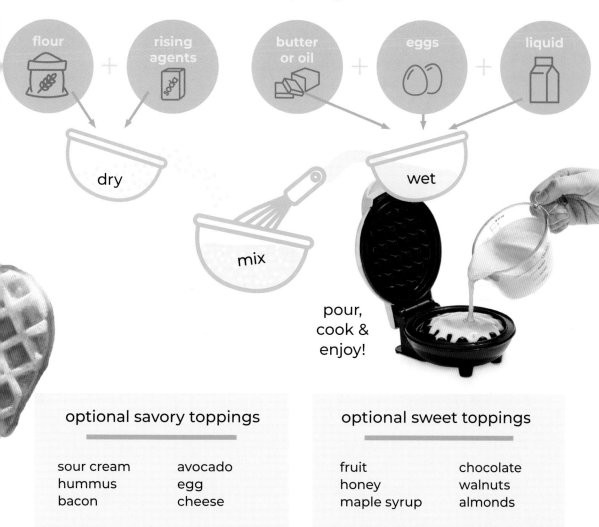

flour + rising agents

butter or oil + eggs + liquid

dry

mix

wet

pour, cook & enjoy!

optional savory toppings	
sour cream	avocado
hummus	egg
bacon	cheese

optional sweet toppings	
fruit	chocolate
honey	walnuts
maple syrup	almonds

TIPS & TRICKS

What's the difference between waffle and pancake batter?

Waffle batter often calls for oil or melted butter whereas pancake batter does not. This alters the fat content, which gives waffles a different texture as a result. You'll notice an airier, fluffier result inside the waffle with a slight crisp on the outside.

How much batter should I use?

For classic waffle or pancake batter, you'll want to add 3.5 tablespoons of batter to your Mini Waffle Maker per waffle. After making hundreds of mini waffles in the Dash kitchen, we've zeroed in on that figure for consistent, perfectly-shaped results.

Are the waffles safe for my dietary restrictions?

We've created a series of nutritional icons so you can easily find the recipes you're looking for. Nutritional icons denote gluten-free, dairy-free, vegan, paleo and nut-free recipes.

gluten free

dairy free

paleo

nut free

vegan

What if I'm gluten-free and I want to make a waffle that isn't marked by a GF icon?

Not a problem! Use the gluten-free waffle recipe, found in the "Classics" section, as your base to the rest of the cookbook's recipes. Additionally, recipes that are already gluten-free are marked by the gluten-free icon.

TOOLS OF THE TINY WAFFLE TRADE

For big success with your mini waffle endeavors, you'll need the following tools:

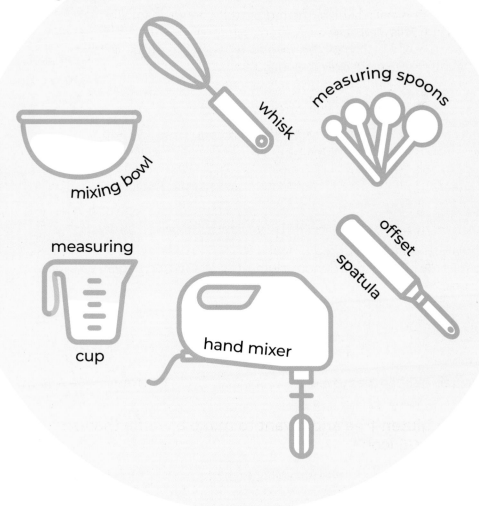

whisk

measuring spoons

mixing bowl

measuring

cup

hand mixer

offset

spatula

AVOIDING COMMON MISTAKES

Don't use the wrong egg size.

Large eggs have approximately 1 ¾ oz. of liquid per egg. If you're using extra-large eggs in a recipe, the ratio of egg in the recipe changes and that may affect your results. We use large eggs in our recipes.

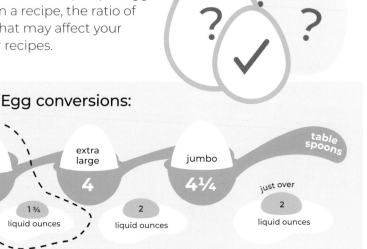

Egg conversions:

medium	*what we use* large	extra large	jumbo	table spoons
3	3½	4	4¼	just over 2
1 ½ liquid ounces	1 ¾ liquid ounces	2 liquid ounces		2 liquid ounces

Substitutions don't react the same way.

moo

We don't know how many times we've read recipe reviews where someone substituted non-dairy milk when the recipe called for dairy milk and then bashed the recipe for not working. Anecdotes like these prove cooking from a recipe can be a double-edged sword — if you don't follow the recipe exactly as written, you may not get the results that you want. See our Tips & Tricks for more info on substitutions for dietary restrictions.

Units of measure shouldn't be altered or overlooked.

In Europe, it's most common to see recipes call for weights instead of teaspoons, tablespoons and cups. That's because those measurements are much more precise but kitchen scales are much less common in the US. Unless instructed to do so, packing the ingredients down into the measuring spoon can adversely affect your results.

Try your hand at the scoop and level!

The best way to measure dry ingredients is the ol' scoop and level method that you may have learned in home economics class. With the scoop and level method, you dip your measuring cup or spoon into the dry ingredients and bring up a heaping, overflowing scoop. Then, using an offset spatula or the back of a knife, sweep the extra powder off the top of the cup and back into the container. To avoid ending up with more of an ingredient than called for, don't tap the cup down on the counter or push the ingredients into the cup.

Tempering is important!

Adding hot melted butter to raw eggs is a good recipe for buttered scrambled eggs, not so much for waffle batter. Instead, when warm ingredients are called for, "temper" them by slowly drizzling them in while mixing so that the eggs are brought up to a warm temperature evenly.

CLASSIC WAFFLES

Classic doesn't mean boring! These recipes have been around since the dawn of breakfast and perfected by Dash, so you'll easily ace the basics of mini waffles. Add inspired ingredients to these classic recipes to make your own flavors.

THE CLASSIC WAFFLE

8-10 waffles • 5 minutes

A traditional, fluffy breakfast favorite topped with maple syrup, whipped cream, powdered sugar and fresh berries. Delicious on their own or with your favorite toppings, this recipe is also the base for some of the fun flavors featured in the other sections of this cookbook.

Ingredients

1 cup all-purpose flour

1 tbsp sugar

2 tsp baking powder

¼ tsp salt

1 large egg

1 cup milk

2 tbsp softened unsalted butter

Directions

1. Mix together the flour, sugar, baking powder and salt in a medium bowl.

2. Whisk together milk, egg and melted butter in a separate bowl. Add the wet ingredients to the dry and mix until just incorporated.

3. Add 3.5 tbsp of batter to your Mini Waffle Maker and cook until golden brown on both sides.

chef tip:

Don't kill the fluffiness! Mix only until no clumps remain.

WHOLE WHEAT WAFFLES

8-10 waffles • 6 minutes

A healthier alternative to standard flour, whole wheat flour means that the bran and germ are left intact when milled, meaning more fiber per waffle! You'll add a bit more butter to this waffle recipe to keep the results moist and delicious.

Ingredients

1 cup whole wheat flour

2 tsp baking powder

2 tbsp sugar

1 large egg

4 tbsp melted salted butter

1 cup whole milk

½ tsp vanilla extract

Directions

1. Whisk together whole wheat flour, sugar and baking powder in a medium bowl.

2. Whisk together eggs, milk and vanilla. Slowly mix in melted butter and stir until smooth. Add wet ingredients to dry ingredients and mix until no clumps remain.

3. Add 4 tbsp of batter to your Mini Waffle Maker and cook until golden brown on both sides.

chef tip:

The quality of your butter and vanilla extract make a big difference.

HAPPY MEDIUM WHOLE WHEAT WAFFLES

8-10 waffles • 6 minutes

This recipe bridges the classic waffle and whole wheat waffle. It contains some whole wheat flour mixed with all-purpose flour and leaves out the sugar for a flavor that's the best of both worlds.

Ingredients

⅓ cup whole wheat flour

⅔ cup all-purpose flour

2 tbsp baking powder

4 tbsp melted unsalted butter

1 large egg

½ cup milk

½ cup seltzer or club soda

Directions

1. Mix together whole wheat flour, all-purpose flour and baking powder in a mixing bowl.

2. Mix together milk, seltzer and egg in a separate bowl. While mixing, slowly drizzle the melted butter into the mix.

3. Add the wet ingredients to the dry ingredients and whisk until no clumps remain. Do not overmix the batter.

4. Add 3.5 tbsp of batter to your Mini Waffle Maker and cook until golden brown on both sides.

chef tip:

Seltzer is a great addition to make waffles come out crispier and lighter.

CHOCOLATE CHIP WAFFLES

8-10 waffles · 5 minutes

Combine crispy batter with gooey chocolate for a perfect combination of flavor and texture. Substitute in dark chocolate chips for a decadent hint of bitterness, or white chocolate chips for waffles that pop.

Ingredients

1 cup all-purpose flour

1 cup chocolate chips

1 tbsp sugar

2 tsp baking powder

¼ tsp salt

1 large egg

1 cup milk

2 tbsp melted unsalted butter

Directions

1. Mix together the flour, sugar, baking powder, chocolate chips and salt in a medium bowl.

2. Whisk together milk, egg and melted butter in a separate bowl. Add the wet ingredients to the dry and mix until just incorporated.

3. Add 3.5 tbsp of batter to your Mini Waffle Maker and cook until golden brown on both sides.

VANILLA YOGURT WAFFLES

8-10 waffles • 7 minutes

This waffle's smooth texture comes from a unique yogurt base and bubbly seltzer, which makes the waffles come out crispier and lighter!

Ingredients

1 ¼ cups all-purpose flour

¼ cups sugar

½ tbsp baking powder

½ tsp kosher salt

1 vanilla bean

1 large egg

2 tbsp vegetable oil

1 cup vanilla Greek yogurt

½ cup seltzer

Directions

1. Mix together flour, baking powder, sugar and salt in a medium bowl.

2. Cut vanilla bean down the middle lengthwise and scrape out the seed paste.

3. Mix together vanilla bean paste, egg, oil and yogurt in a separate bowl.

4. Add the dry ingredients into the wet a little at a time while mixing. Once all the ingredients are incorporated, mix in the seltzer.

5. Add 3.5 tbsp of batter to your Mini Waffle Maker and cook until golden brown on both sides.

BUTTERMILK WAFFLES

with buttermilk syrup

8-10 waffles · 10 minutes

Crispy on the outside and soft on the inside, these buttermilk waffles are complemented by sweet, gooey homemade buttermilk syrup. These waffles have an ideal fluff that will become a staple in your kitchen.

Ingredients

1 cup all-purpose flour

1 tbsp sugar

1 tsp baking powder

1/2 tsp baking soda

1/2 tsp salt

1 cup buttermilk

2 tbsp melted unsalted butter

1 large egg

1 tsp vanilla extract

For Buttermilk Syrup

1 cup sugar

½ cup buttermilk

1 stick unsalted butter

¼ tsp salt

1 tsp baking soda

1 tsp vanilla extract

Directions for Waffles

1. Mix together flour, sugar, baking powder, baking soda and salt in a medium bowl.

2. Whisk together egg, buttermilk, vanilla and melted butter in a separate bowl.

3. Combine wet ingredients with the dry ingredients and whisk until just incorporated.

4. Add 3.5 tbsp of batter to your Mini Waffle Maker and cook until golden brown on both sides.

Directions for Buttermilk Syrup

1. Heat sugar, buttermilk and butter in a pan over medium heat until a noticeable boil begins.

2. Boil for 2 minutes and remove from heat.

3. Mix in baking soda, salt and vanilla.

chef tip:

Yogurt thinned with milk can be a substitute for buttermilk.

GLUTEN FREE WAFFLES

8-10 waffles • 5 minutes

A gluten-free version of the classic waffle that's just as tasty! This recipe can easily be incorporated as a base for other types of waffles. Try it with berries, chocolate chips, and more!

Ingredients

½ cup oat flour

½ cup almond meal

1 tsp baking powder

⅓ cup white sugar

1 large egg

½ cup whole milk

2 tbsp canola oil

Directions

1. Whisk together oat flour, almond meal, baking powder and sugar.

2. Whisk together egg, milk and oil until smooth. Combine wet ingredients with the dry ingredients and mix until no clumps remain.

3. Add 3.5 tbsp of waffle mix to your Mini Waffle Maker and cook until golden brown on both sides.

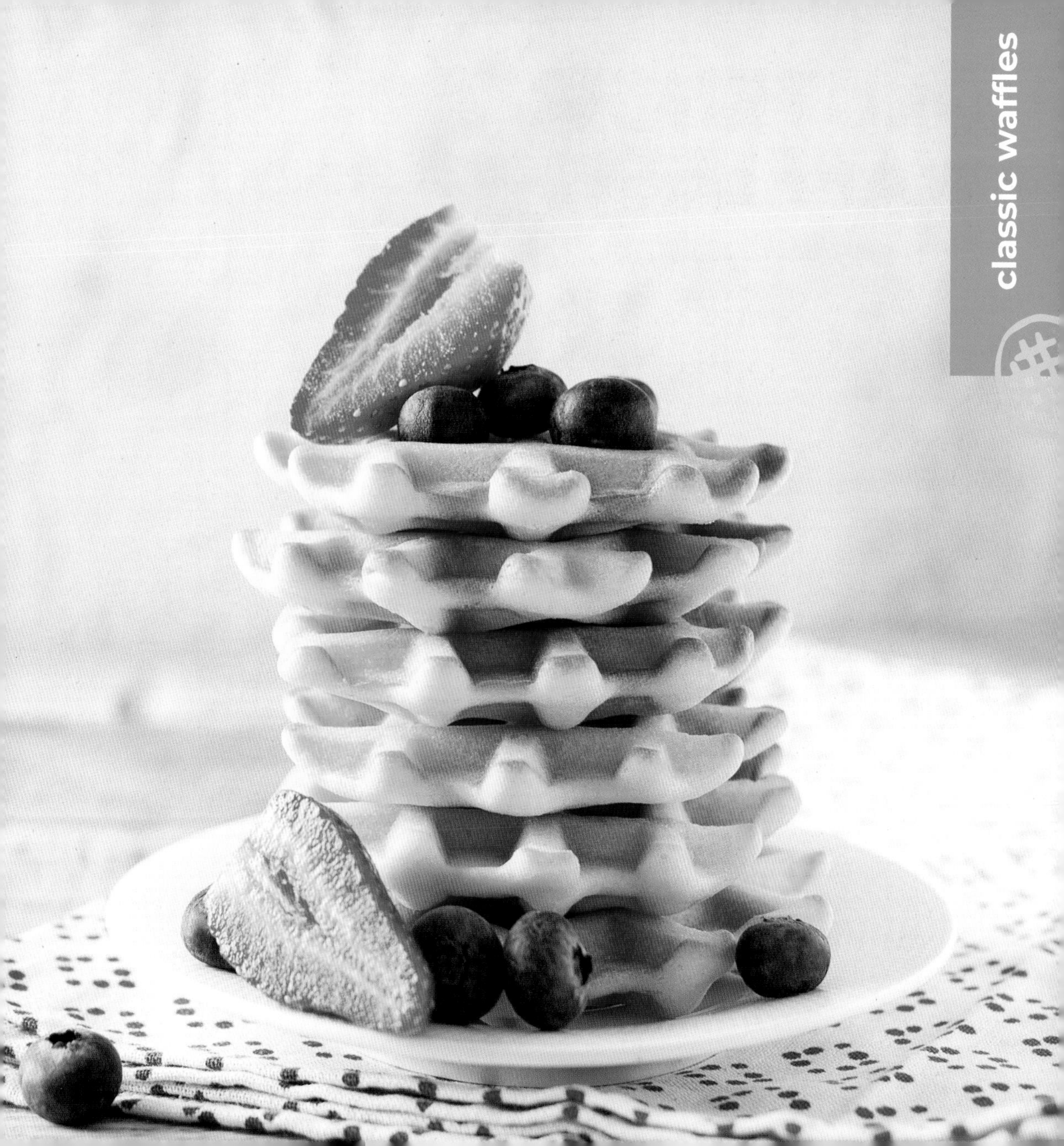

PROTEIN WAFFLES

7-9 waffles • 6 minutes

If you're looking for a creative way to add protein to your diet, you've come to the right place. You can even use different flavors of powder to add hints of chocolate, vanilla, milkshake and more.

Ingredients

1 cup all-purpose flour

¼ cup protein powder

1 tbsp sugar

2 tsp baking powder

¼ tsp salt

1 large egg

1 cup milk

2 tbsp melted unsalted butter

Directions

1. Mix together flour, sugar, baking powder, protein powder and salt in a medium bowl.

2. Whisk together milk, egg and melted butter in a separate bowl. Add the wet ingredients to the dry and mix until just incorporated.

3. Add 3.5 tbsp of batter to your Mini Waffle Maker and cook until golden brown on both sides.

chef tip:

Add or subtract protein powder from the suggested quantity to your liking!

CLASSIC VANILLA KETO WAFFLES

8-10 waffles • 6 minutes

Almond flour, coconut flour and a dash of vanilla make these waffles a delicious way to stick to a keto plan while enjoying a sweet treat.

Ingredients

4 large eggs

⅔ cup heavy cream

2 tbsp unsalted butter, melted and cooled

1 tsp vanilla extract

1 cup superfine almond flour

¼ cup coconut flour

2 tsp baking powder

⅓ cup monkfruit sweetener

¼ tsp kosher salt

Directions

1. Whisk together eggs with heavy cream, melted butter and vanilla extract until smooth.

2. Add almond flour, coconut flour, baking powder, monkfruit and salt. Mix thoroughly until smooth.

3. Spoon 2 Tbsp of batter onto waffle maker, and cook until golden brown and cooked through.

BELGIAN LIÈGE WAFFLES

6-8 waffles · 6 minutes

Belgian pearl sugar creates a crisp, sugary crunch in these sweet, doughy waffles inspired by traditional Belgian cooking. A pinch of salt and cinnamon adds a touch of spice for perfectly balanced flavor and texture.

Ingredients

1 cup flour

½ packet dry yeast

¼ cup lukewarm milk

6 tbsp unsalted butter

1 large egg

1 tsp vanilla extract

1 tsp honey

½ cup Belgian pearl sugar

Pinch of salt

Pinch of cinnamon

Directions

1. Dissolve yeast in lukewarm milk in a small bowl.

2. Mix together flour, milk mixture, butter, egg, vanilla extract, honey, cinnamon and salt in a separate bowl. Let the dough rise until it doubles in size. This takes about 30 minutes.

3. Slowly mix in the sugar. Divide batter into small 2-inch patties.

4. Add patty to your Mini Waffle Maker and cook until golden brown on both sides.

chef tip:

Don't have Belgian pearl sugar? Break sugar cubes into pieces instead!

HONEY WAFFLES

7-9 waffles · 6 minutes

The sweetest classic of them all, honey waffles combine almond milk with honey and safflower oil for a flavor that will have you all abuzz!

Ingredients

¾ cup almond milk

1 large egg

2 tbsp safflower oil

1 tbsp honey

¾ cup whole wheat flour

1 tsp baking powder

Directions

1. Whisk together flour and baking powder.

2. Whisk almond milk, egg, safflower oil and honey together. Add the wet ingredients to the dry and mix until well-combined.

3. Add 3 tbsp of batter to your Mini Waffle Maker and cook until golden brown on both sides. Serve with additional honey, if desired.

chef tip:

Almond milk does a great job of enhancing this recipe's flavor.

BLUEBERRY MUFFIN WAFFLES

8-10 waffles • 6 minutes

A farm-to-table favorite, the tang of fresh blueberries pairs wonderfully with the sweetness of our classic waffle batter. The perfect way to sneak just a little bit of fruit into your morning routine.

Ingredients

1 ½ cup all-purpose flour

⅔ cup white sugar

1 tsp baking powder

¼ tsp kosher salt

1 large egg

½ cup whole milk

4 tbsp canola oil

½ cup blueberries

Directions

1. Whisk together flour, sugar, baking powder and salt in a medium bowl.

2. Whisk together egg, milk and oil. Add in dry ingredients and mix until smooth. Fold in blueberries.

3. Add 3 tbsp of waffle mix to your Mini Waffle Maker and cook until golden brown on both sides. Serve with additional blueberries and syrup, if desired.

chef tip:

Cane sugar is best to use here, as it ideally complements fresh blueberries.

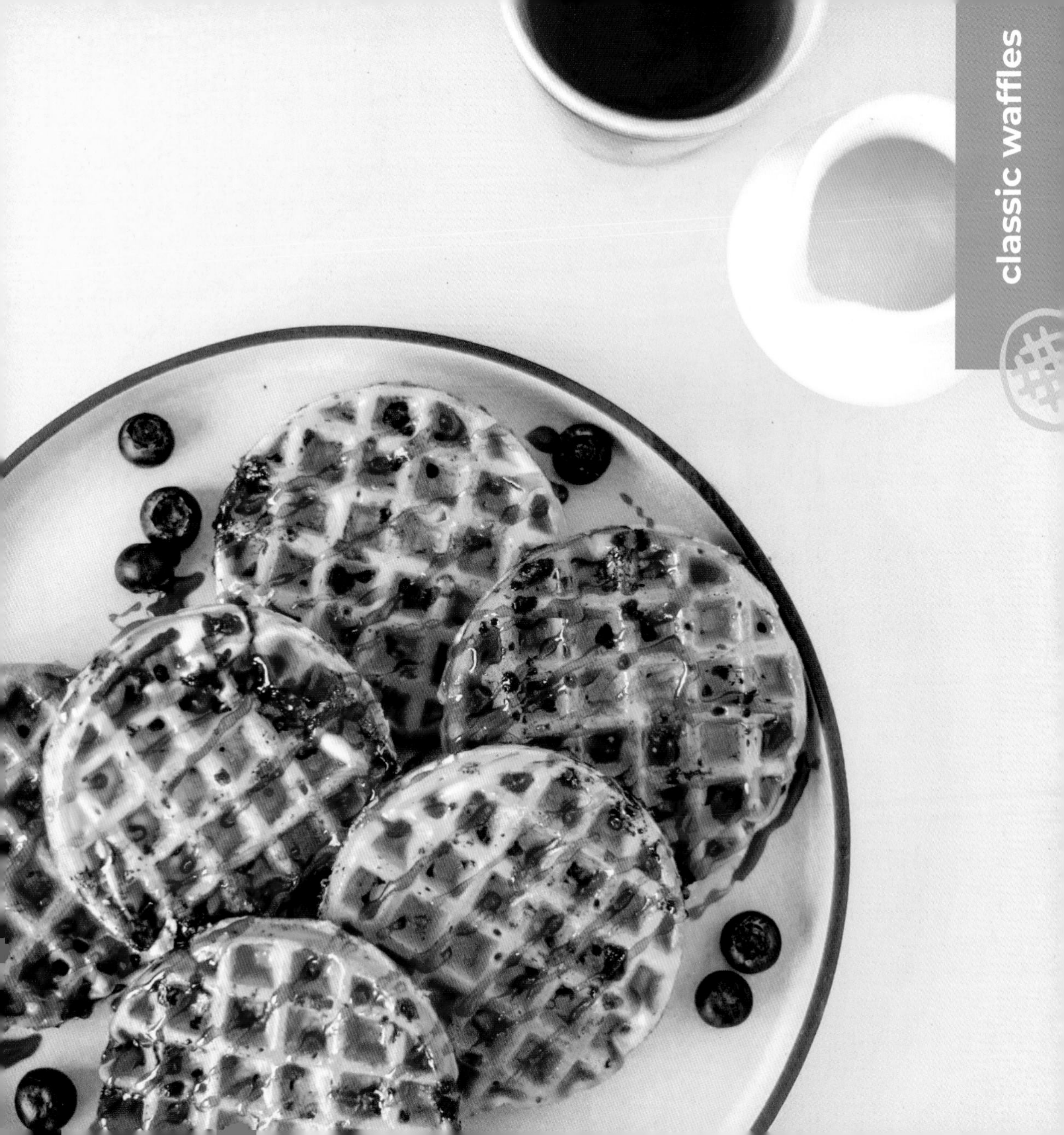

ALMOND MILK WAFFLES

8-10 waffles · 6 minutes

Perfect for those with a sensitivity to lactose, these waffles substitute in delicious almond milk for a light, mild flavor and fluffy texture.

Ingredients

1 cup whole wheat flour

½ tbsp baking powder

⅛ tsp salt

1 large egg, separated

¾ cup almond milk

1 tbsp safflower oil

1 tbsp maple syrup

½ tsp vanilla extract

Toppings

Strawberries

Blueberries

Maple syrup

Chocolate sauce

Directions

1. Mix together flour, baking powder and salt.

2. Beat egg white until light and fluffy. Whisk together egg yolk, almond milk, maple syrup, vanilla and safflower oil in a separate bowl. Mix the yolk mixture with the dry ingredients. Slowly fold in whipped egg white.

3. Add 3.5 tbsp of batter to your Mini Waffle Maker and cook until golden brown on both sides. Top with fruit, chocolate drizzle and maple syrup, if desired.

PALEO WAFFLES

4-5 waffles • 5 minutes

Paleo waffles are here! These waffles showcase breakfast flavors like banana and vanilla in a new way and are perfect for the paleo lifestyle.

Ingredients

2 large eggs

½ banana, mashed

¾ tsp maple syrup

½ tsp vanilla extract

½ tsp baking powder

¼ cup almond flour

1 ½ tbsp coconut flour

Pinch of salt

Directions for Waffles

1. Mix together eggs, banana, vanilla extract and maple syrup in a small bowl.

2. Whisk together dry ingredients in a separate bowl. Add the wet ingredients to the dry and mix until just incorporated.

3. Add 3.5 tbsp of batter to your Mini Waffle Maker and cook until golden brown on both sides.

SWEET WAFFLES

A collection of waffles that'll satisfy any sweet tooth and send your dentist running for the hills. From chocolate strawberry waffles to fudge brownies and pumpkin spice, this section will dazzle any dessert devotee.

PUMPKIN SPICE WAFFLES

8-10 waffles · 15 minutes

Drop the latte and get your fix of pumpkin spice from these delicious fall waffles instead! Lovers of pumpkin pie can turn to this waffle recipe during any season for a sweet, flavorful treat.

Ingredients

1 cup all-purpose flour

1 tsp baking powder

1 tbsp pumpkin pie spice

¼ cup sugar

Pinch of salt

2 large eggs

½ cup whole milk

⅜ cup canned pumpkin

¾ cup unsalted butter

½ tsp vanilla extract

Directions

1. Melt butter on a small pan over low heat. Shut off heat so butter is not hot when added to the mix.

2. Mix together the dry ingredients and set aside.

3. Add eggs into a bowl and beat with a whisk. Add milk, pumpkin, melted butter and vanilla, mix to incorporate.

spice it up!

Make pumpkin-shaped waffles with the Dash Pumpkin Mini Waffle Maker.

4. Add dry ingredients into wet in three rounds, fully incorporate all dry ingredients before added the next round.

5. Add 3.5 tbsp of waffle mix to your Mini Waffle Maker and cook until golden brown on both sides.

chef tip:

Make pumpkin pie spice with cinnamon, ginger, nutmeg & cloves.

BANANA BREAD WAFFLES

12-14 waffles • 6 minutes

Mashed bananas and a buttermilk waffle base make this sweet treat a great snack or dessert. This combination of a nutrient-packed star ingredient and buttermilk waffles is a breakfast opportunity worth seizing.

Ingredients

1 ½ cups all-purpose flour

1 tsp baking powder

¼ tsp baking soda

¼ tsp kosher salt

1 cup mashed bananas
(roughly 2 bananas)

¾ cup buttermilk

¼ cup light brown sugar

2 large eggs

3 tbsp canola oil

Directions

1. Whisk together flour, baking powder, baking soda and salt in a medium bowl.

2. Mash bananas with a fork or place in stand mixer with paddle attachment until no large chunks remain. Add buttermilk, brown sugar, eggs and oil. Whisk until well-combined. Add dry ingredients and mix until no clumps remain.

3. Add 3 tbsp of batter to your Mini Waffle Maker and cook until golden brown on both sides. Serve with additional bananas, honey and powdered sugar, if desired.

APPLE CINNAMON WAFFLES

10-12 waffles · 15 minutes

Fans of apple crumble will fall in love with these waffled apple cinnamon treats! Shredded apple and lemon juice create a zesty treat that is perfect served piping hot with a side of cool ice cream.

Ingredients

3 large apples, grated and squeezed dry

1 tbsp lemon juice

⅓ cup whole wheat flour

1 tsp baking powder

1 tbsp brown sugar

½ tsp cinnamon

¼ tsp salt

2 large eggs

Directions

1. Toss grated apple with lemon juice and set aside.

2. Stir flour, baking powder, sugar, cinnamon and salt together. Sprinkle over the apples, tossing to coat.

3. Whisk eggs together and add them to apple mixture, mixing to coat evenly.

4. Add 3 tbsp of batter to your Mini Waffle Maker and cook until golden brown on both sides.

chef tip:

Serve with ice cream or yogurt for a cool complement!

CHOCO-HAZELNUT WAFFLES

6-8 waffles · 6 minutes

If you're anything like us, you've got a serious Nutella® addiction. These waffles are the perfect fix to your cravings: top them with even more Nutella® for a deliciously indulgent treat!

Ingredients

1 cup all-purpose flour

2 tbsp Nutella®

2 tsp baking powder

¼ tsp salt

1 large egg

1 cup milk

2 tbsp melted unsalted butter

Directions

1. Mix together the flour, baking powder and salt in a medium bowl.

2. Whisk together milk, egg and melted butter and Nutella® in a separate bowl. Add the wet ingredients to the dry and mix until just incorporated.

3. Add 3.5 tbsp of batter to your Mini Waffle Maker and cook until golden brown on both sides.

SOUR CREAM CHOCOLATE CHIP WAFFLES

10-12 waffles · 8 minutes

We've upgraded classic chocolate chip waffles with a dash of sour cream for added moisture and a touch of savory flavor to balance the sweetness.

Ingredients

½ cup sour cream

2 tbsp whole milk

2 tbsp melted unsalted butter

1 large egg

½ tsp vanilla extract

¾ cup all-purpose flour

1 tsp baking powder

¼ tsp baking soda

⅛ tsp salt

1 tbsp sugar

½ cup mini chocolate chips

Directions

1. Whisk together sour cream, milk, melted butter, egg and vanilla.

2. Whisk the flour baking powder, baking soda, salt and sugar. Add the wet ingredients to the dry and stir until just combined. Gently fold in chocolate chips.

3. Add 3 tbsp of batter to your Mini Waffle Maker and cook until golden brown on both sides.

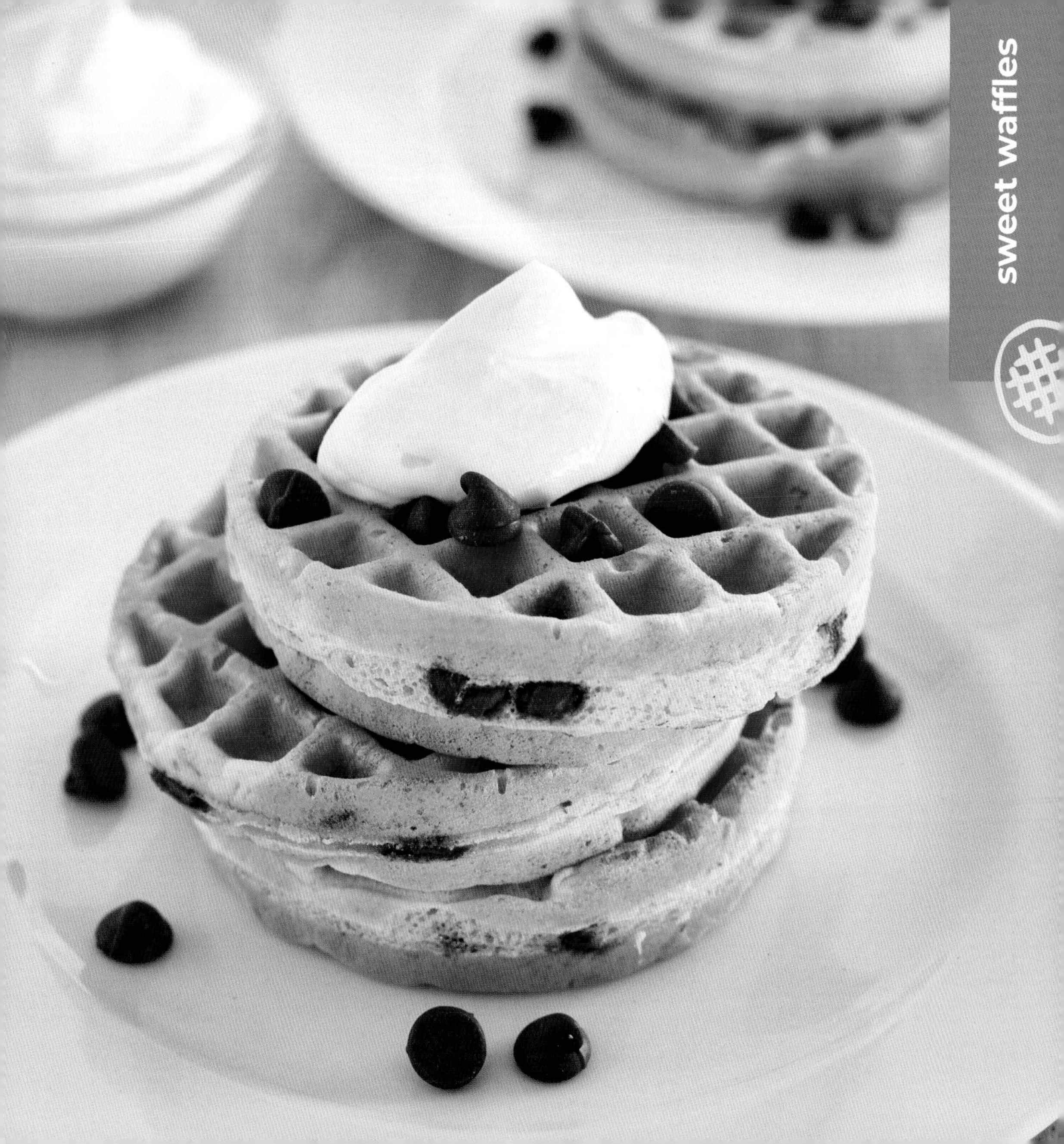

WAFFLED CARROT CAKE

10-12 waffles · 6 minutes

Our recipe includes all of the nuts and spices of the traditional carrot cake, but made right on your countertop. Finish with your favorite frosting.

Ingredients

½ cup all-purpose flour

½ cup light brown sugar

½ tsp baking powder

⅛ tsp baking soda

⅛ tsp cinnamon

⅛ tsp ground clove

⅛ tsp nutmeg

1 large egg

¼ cup buttermilk

¼ cup whole milk

½ tsp vanilla extract

½ cup shredded carrot

3 tbsp raisins

3 tbsp chopped walnuts

Directions

1. Mix together flour, sugar, baking powder, baking soda, cinnamon, clove and nutmeg.

2. Whisk together egg, buttermilk, milk and vanilla extract until smooth. Add in dry ingredients and mix until no clumps remain. Mix in carrot, raisins and walnuts.

3. Add 3 tbsp of waffle mix to your Mini Waffle Maker and cook until golden brown on both sides.

chef tip:

Avoid overcooking this waffle to preserve moisture.

SNICKERDOODLE WAFFLES

10-12 waffles · 10 minutes

Meet the waffled version of everybody's favorite cinnamon sugar cookies, topped with a simple garnish for the ideal cookie-like texture.

Ingredients

2 cups all-purpose flour

2 tsp kosher salt

4 tsp baking powder

⅓ cup sugar

4 tsp cinnamon

3 tsp cream of tartar

2 large eggs

1 ½ cups milk

⅓ cup unsalted butter

2 tsp vanilla extract

For Cinnamon Sugar Garnish

¼ cup granulated white sugar

1 tbsp ground cinnamon

Directions

1. In a small pan over low heat, combine milk and butter. Stir until milk is warm and butter is melted.

2. Mix together flour, salt, baking powder, sugar, cinnamon and cream of tartar in a large bowl.

3. Whisk together eggs and vanilla. Slowly pour in the warmed milk and butter.

4. Pour dry ingredients into the wet in three stages, incorporating all dry ingredients before adding the next.

5. Add 3.5 tbsp of waffle mix to your Mini Waffle Maker and cook until golden brown on both sides.

6. Remove waffle and set on a wire rack and sprinkle with cinnamon sugar garnish.

snow good!

Make snowflake waffles
with our Snowflake
Mini Waffle Maker.

CHOCO-STRAWBERRY WAFFLES

7-9 waffles • 6 minutes

The tartness of strawberries and the sweetness of chocolate balance perfectly, for a dessert waffle that's difficult to resist.

Ingredients

½ cup whole wheat flour

2 tbsp cocoa powder

1 tbsp coconut sugar

½ tsp baking powder

¼ tsp baking soda

1 ½ tbsp mini chocolate chips

1 large egg

½ cup Greek yogurt

¼ cup almond milk

½ tsp vanilla extract

Toppings

Melted dark chocolate

Sliced strawberries

Directions

1. Whisk together flour, cocoa powder, coconut sugar, baking powder, baking soda and mini chocolate chips.

2. Combine egg, Greek yogurt, almond milk and vanilla extract in another bowl. Add this mixture to the dry ingredients and mix until just combined.

3. Add 3.5 tbsp of batter to your Mini Waffle Maker and cook until golden brown on both sides. Serve with sliced strawberries and a dark chocolate drizzle, if desired.

chef tip:

If the waffles don't rise, add a splash of seltzer to the batter.

DARK CHOCOLATE WAFFLES

8-10 waffles · 6 minutes

A bittersweet variation of a basic chocolate waffle, topped with all the components of a heavenly dark chocolate dessert.

Ingredients

¾ cup all-purpose flour

3 tbsp white granulated sugar

¼ cup cocoa powder

½ tsp baking powder

¼ tsp baking soda

½ tsp kosher or sea salt

1 large egg

2 tbsp melted unsalted butter

1 cup buttermilk

1 tsp vanilla extract

¼ cup semi sweet mini chocolate chips

Optional Toppings:

Vanilla ice cream

Sliced fruit

Whipped cream

Powdered sugar

continued on next page ⟶

Dark Chocolate Waffles continued...

Directions

1. In a small pan over low heat, melt the butter. Shut off heat so butter is not hot when added to the mix.

2. Mix together the dry ingredients and set aside.

3. Beat egg with a whisk. Mix in buttermilk, butter and vanilla.

4. Add dry ingredients into wet in three rounds. Fully incorporate all dry ingredients before adding the next round. Fold in the chocolate chips.

5. Add 3.5 tbsp of batter to your Mini Waffle Maker and cook until golden brown on both sides.

chef tip:

Add an additional ½ tsp of vanilla extract if the waffle is too bitter.

PEANUT BUTTER WAFFLE TOWER

10-12 waffles • 6 minutes

Stack these sweet peanut butter waffles for a stunning breakfast or dessert! Chocolate peanut butter glaze holds waffles together into a decadent tower.

Ingredients

1 cup all-purpose flour

1 ½ tsp baking powder

1 cup almond milk

1 large egg

2 tbsp safflower oil

¼ cup smooth peanut butter

For Chocolate Peanut Butter Glaze

½ cup dark chocolate chips

2 tsp coconut oil

¼ cup chopped peanuts

Directions

1. Mix together flour and baking powder.

2. Whisk together milk, oil, egg and peanut butter in a separate bowl. Add the wet ingredients to the dry and mix until just incorporated.

3. Add 3 tbsp of batter to your Mini Waffle Maker and cook until golden brown on both sides.

4. In the microwave, melt together chocolate chips and coconut oil 10 seconds at a time. Stir until consistency is soft.

5. Layer 4-6 waffles with glaze between each layer. Top with additional glaze, peanuts and chocolate chips.

VEGAN LEMON WAFFLES

8-10 waffles • 6 minutes

Delicious vegan waffles with a lemon twist add zest to wake you up the right way! These healthy waffles pack a flavorful punch.

Ingredients

1 cup spelt flour

1 tsp baking soda

¾ cup almond milk

1 lemon, zested and juiced

2 tbsp safflower oil

1 tbsp ground flax seed

3 tbsp water

2 tbsp maple syrup

Directions

1. Mix spelt flour with baking soda.

2. Whisk together the almond milk, lemon juice and zest, safflower oil, flax seed, water and maple syrup in a separate bowl. Add the wet ingredients to the dry and mix until just incorporated.

3. Add 3.5 tbsp of batter to your Mini Waffle Maker and cook until golden brown on both sides.

SWEET CHAFFLES

8-10 waffles · 6 minutes

Hop on the chaffle trend with this delicious almond and vanilla snack. An ideal healthy way to treat yourself after a long day!

Ingredients

2 large eggs

2 large egg yolks

2 tbsp unsalted butter, melted

1 cup shredded mozzarella cheese

½ tsp baking powder

2 tbsp monk fruit sweetener

2 tbsp superfine almond flour

2 tsp vanilla extract

½ tsp almond extract (optional)

1 dash kosher salt

Directions

1. In medium bowl, whisk together eggs with egg yolks until frothy.

2. In separate medium bowl, combine butter with mozzarella and mash until well mixed.

3. Pour mozzarella mixture into egg mixture and add baking powder, monkfruit, almond flour, vanilla extract, almond extract and kosher salt. Whisk until evenly combined.

4. Add 3 tbsp of batter to your Mini Waffle Maker and cook until golden brown on both sides.

COOKIES N' CREAM WAFFLES

6-8 waffles · 6 minutes

With tasty chocolate cookie bits scattered throughout, these Cookies 'N Cream Waffles boast the perfect balance of crunch and fluff. Best when washed down with a gulp of milk!

Ingredients

½ cup pulverized Oreo® cookies (approximately 6 cookies)

1 cup all-purpose flour

2 tsp baking powder

1 tbsp white sugar

1 large egg

1 cup whole milk

Directions

1. Mix together pulverized Oreos®, flour, baking powder and sugar.

2. Whisk together eggs and milk until smooth. Add dry ingredients and mix until no clumps remain.

3. Add 3.5 tbsp of batter to your Mini Waffle Maker and cook until golden brown on both sides. Serve with additional Oreos® if desired.

RED VELVET WAFFLES

10-12 waffles • 6 minutes

A red velvet spin on the buttermilk waffle makes it the perfect base for frosting or ice cream, or just as a decadent stand-alone treat that tastes as good as it looks!

Ingredients

2 cups all-purpose flour

¼ cup white granulated sugar

¼ cup cocoa powder

1 tsp baking powder

½ tsp baking soda

½ tsp cinnamon

1 tsp salt

1 ¾ cups buttermilk

2 large eggs

¼ cup unsalted butter

2 tsp vanilla extract

1 tbsp red food coloring

Directions

1. In a small pan over low heat, melt butter. Shut off heat so butter is not hot when added to the mix.

2. Mix together the dry ingredients and set aside.

3. Beat eggs in a bowl. Slowly stir in buttermilk, butter, vanilla and food coloring.

4. Mix dry ingredients into wet in three rounds. Fully incorporate all dry ingredients before adding the next round.

5. Add 3.5 tbsp of batter to your Mini Waffle Maker and cook until golden brown on both sides.

lovin' it!

Make heart waffles with our Heart Mini Waffle Maker.

MATCHA MOCHI WAFFLES

8-10 waffles • 6 minutes

Great for parties and gatherings, this waffle features the key ingredient in green tea. Inspired by matcha powder's antioxidants, this waffle takes the guilt out of snacking.

Ingredients

1 ½ cups sweet (glutinous) rice flour

1 tbsp matcha powder

½ cup white sugar

1 ½ tsp baking powder

1 large egg

1 cup whole milk

3 tbsp canola oil

Directions

1. Whisk together sweet rice flour, matcha powder, white sugar and baking powder.

2. Whisk together egg, milk and oil until smooth. Add dry ingredients and mix until no clumps remain.

3. Add 3.5 tbsp of waffle mix to your Mini Waffle Maker and cook until golden brown on both sides. Serve with additional dusting of matcha powder and powdered sugar, if desired.

chef tip:

The amount of matcha you use may determine the color of your waffles.

PUMPKIN BROWNIE WAFFLES

8-10 waffles • 6 minutes

These waffles are a brownie version of their fellow pumpkin spice rendition. Perfect for autumn or for chocolate lovers seeking a delightful seasonal kick.

Ingredients

2 tbsp almond butter

⅓ cup coconut sugar

6 tbsp almond flour

1 tbsp flax seed

3 tbsp water

½ tsp vanilla

½ cup pumpkin purée

¼ cup cocoa powder

½ tsp cinnamon

⅛ tsp nutmeg

¼ tsp pimento

¼ tsp baking powder

¼ cup mini chocolate chips

Pinch of salt

Directions

1. Mix together almond butter and coconut sugar Add flax, water and vanilla.

2. Mix in pumpkin, cocoa powder, almond flour, baking powder, salt and spices. Fold in chocolate chips.

3. Add 3.5 tbsp of batter to your Mini Waffle Maker and bake until cooked through.

spice it up!

Make pumpkin waffles with the Dash Pumpkin Mini Waffle Maker.

TRIPLE FUDGE BROWNIE WAFFLES

10-12 waffles • 6 minutes

Love the corner brownies fresh from the pan? Now the entire brownie is a corner piece, baked right in your own Mini Waffle Maker!

Ingredients

6 tbsp bittersweet chocolate

2 tbsp unsweetened chocolate

¾ stick unsalted butter

¾ cup sugar

1 tsp vanilla extract

2 large eggs

½ tsp salt

½ cup all-purpose flour

½ cup mini chocolate chips

Toppings

Chopped walnuts

Shredded coconut

Directions

1. Melt chocolate and butter and mix together until smooth. In a medium bowl, whisk together eggs, sugar and vanilla extract.

2. Add egg mixture to chocolate and mix until no clumps remain. Stir in salt and flour until just combined. Fold in chocolate chips.

3. Add 3.5 tbsp of batter to your Mini Waffle Maker and cook.

chef tip:

For a better crunch, mix chopped walnuts into the batter.

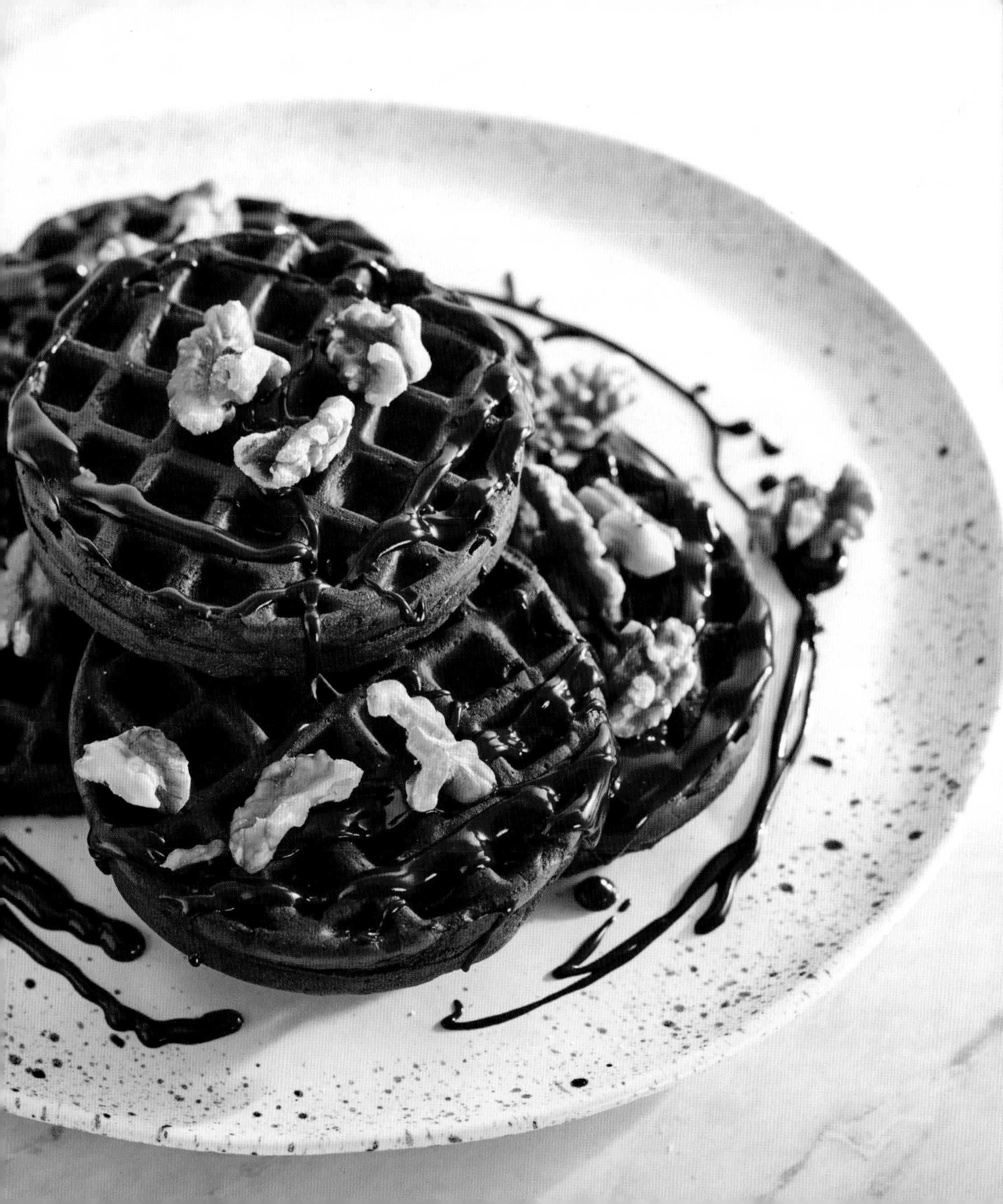

CINNAMON ROLL WAFFLES

10-12 waffles · 15 minutes

Sweet cinnamon roll waffles are a perfect treat, and our cream cheese icing is the ideal, melt-y topper to satisfy your sweet tooth.

Ingredients

1 cup all-purpose flour

1 tbsp sugar

1 tsp baking powder

½ tsp baking soda

½ tsp salt

1 cup buttermilk

2 tbsp unsalted melted butter

1 large egg

1 tsp vanilla extract

3 tsp cinnamon

For Cream Cheese Icing

2 tbsp melted unsalted butter

2 tbsp softened cream cheese

½ cup powdered sugar

1 tsp vanilla extract

3 tbsp whole milk

chef tip:

Allow the waffles to cool before spreading icing to prevent it from melting.

Directions

1. Whisk together flour, sugar, baking powder, baking soda and salt in a medium bowl.

2. Whisk together the egg, buttermilk, ½ tsp vanilla extract and melted butter in a separate bowl.

3. Combine the wet ingredients with the dry ingredients and whisk until combined. Stir in the cinnamon and ½ tsp of vanilla extract.

4. Add 3.5 tbsp of batter to your Mini Waffle Maker and cook until golden brown on both sides. Drizzle warm cream cheese icing over cinnamon roll waffles.

For Cream Cheese Icing

1. Whisk together butter and cream cheese in a medium bowl. Stir in the powdered sugar, vanilla extract and milk.

LEMON POPPY WAFFLES

7-9 waffles • 8 minutes

It's hard to go wrong with a lemon poppy bundt cake with an icing glaze, but if you're like us, you find it hard to stop at one slice. Instead, get your lemon poppy fix with these delicious waffles you can enjoy any time!

Ingredients

1 cup all-purpose flour

1 tbsp sugar

2 tsp baking powder

¼ tsp salt

1 large egg

1 cup milk

2 tbsp softened unsalted butter

2 tbsp lemon curd

1 tbsp poppy seeds

1 lemon, zested

For Lemon Glaze

1 cup confectioners sugar

3 tbsp lemon juice

chef tip:

Add more sugar to the glaze to thicken, or more juice for a thinner consistency.

continued on next page ⟶

Lemon Poppy Waffles continued...

Directions

1. Mix together flour, sugar, baking powder, salt and poppy seeds in a medium bowl. Zest the lemon and add to bowl.

2. Whisk together milk, egg and melted butter and lemon curd in a separate bowl. Add the wet ingredients to the dry and mix until well-incorporated.

3. Add 3.5 tbsp of batter to your Mini Waffle Maker and cook until golden brown on both sides.

For Lemon Glaze

1. Mix together confectioners sugar with lemon juice.

2. Drizzle over the top of the waffle in a zig-zag pattern.

VEGAN CHOCOLATE WAFFLES

10-12 waffles · 6 minutes

These waffles are a decadent chocolate escape, with rich cocoa powder and maple syrup combining to create a moist, flavorful treat that is 100% vegan.

Ingredients

1 ½ cups whole wheat flour

⅓ cup cocoa powder

3 tbsp maple syrup

1 ½ cups almond milk

3 tbsp melted coconut oil

¼ tsp salt

Directions

1. Mix together flour, cocoa powder and salt in a small bowl.

2. Mix together maple syrup, almond milk and coconut oil in a separate bowl. Add the wet ingredients to the dry and mix until just incorporated.

3. Add 3.5 tbsp of batter to your Mini Waffle Maker and bake until cooked through.

AVOCADO BROWNIE WAFFLES

8-10 waffles • 10 minutes

A fudge waffle with a hint of avocado and coconut instead of large eggs. This blend of banana, coconut and avocado makes for a healthier result that maintains moist, fudge-like flavor.

Ingredients

3 tbsp ground flax seed

½ cup water

1 large avocado, peeled and pitted

1 large banana

1 tsp almond extract

½ cup cocoa powder

1 tsp baking powder

¾ cup coconut sugar

½ cup coconut flour

Directions

1. Using a high-powered blender, blend together flax, avocado, banana and almond extract until smooth. Add the remaining ingredients and blend on low power.

2. Add 3.5 tbsp of batter to your Mini Waffle Maker and bake until cooked through.

OATMEAL CHOCOLATE CHIP WAFFLES

6-8 waffles · 15 minutes

Nothing says breakfast like warm oatmeal, the fluff of the classic waffle and the indulgence of gooey chocolate chips. Now, you can have them all in one waffle!

Ingredients

1 cup gluten free oats

1 tsp baking powder

½ tsp cinnamon

2 tbsp ground flax seed

2 bananas

⅔ cup almond milk

1 tbsp maple syrup

⅓ cup mini chocolate chips

Toppings

Sliced banana

Whipped cream

Maple syrup

Directions

1. Using a high-powered blender, blend all ingredients except the chocolate chips. Fold chocolate chips into blended batter.

2. Add 3.5 tbsp of batter to your Mini Waffle Maker and cook until golden brown on both sides. Top with sliced banana, maple syrup and whipped cream, if desired.

BEACH COCONUT WAFFLES

5-7 waffles • 6 minutes

Kick back, relax and enjoy the tropical taste of these mini waffles! Coconut oil is high in healthy saturated fats, so not only are these waffles the ideal morning getaway, they're also great for you.

Ingredients

2 large eggs

1 banana

½ cup shredded coconut

1 tsp vanilla

1 tsp cinnamon

1 ½ tsp coconut oil

Toppings

Shaved coconut

Coconut cream

Fresh berries

Honey drizzle

Directions

1. Mix all ingredients together in a large bowl until consistency is smooth.

2. Add 3.5 tbsp of batter to your Mini Waffle Maker and cook until golden brown on both sides. Top with shaved coconut and coconut cream.

3. Garnish with berries and honey, if desired.

chef tip:

If the batter is too thick, add a splash of water!

SAVORY
WAFFLES

A series of umami-packed ideas that bring out
the savory side of mini waffles. Packed with
global recipes like curry waffles and waffled
falafel, these flavor-packed creations make for
tasty snacks and delicious mini meals.

BRITTANY-STYLE BUCKWHEAT WAFFLES

11-13 waffles · 6 minutes

A waffle variant on buckwheat crêpes, perfect for a French-inspired breakfast.

Ingredients

1 cup buckwheat flour

1 ½ tsp baking powder

1 tsp baking soda

2 large eggs, separated

4 tbsp melted salted butter

1 cup skim milk

¼ cup water

Pinch of sea salt

Directions

1. Mix together buckwheat flour, baking powder, baking soda and salt in a large bowl.

2. Beat egg whites until fluffy and make stiff peaks when the beaters are lifted and set aside.

3. Whisk together the yolks, milk, melted butter and water in a medium bowl. Add the wet ingredients to the dry ingredients and mix until well-combined. Fold egg whites into the batter.

4. Add 3.5 tbsp of batter to your Mini Waffle Maker and cook until golden brown on both sides.

chef tip:

Top with shredded gruyére, a slice of ham and a fried egg for a fabulous brunch.

THANKSGIVING WAFFLES

10-12 waffles • 10 minutes

Easily made with leftover stuffing, this waffle brings the best of Thanksgiving packed in a compact waffle snack. Top with cranberry sauce, turkey, or gravy for a bite of autumn during any season!

Ingredients

2 cups stuffing

1 large egg

2 tbsp chicken stock (more as needed)

Cranberry sauce, gravy, turkey for toppings

Directions

1. Mix stuffing with egg and add chicken stock until batter is moist.

2. Add 3.5 tbsp of batter to your Mini Waffle Maker and cook until golden brown on both sides. Top with cranberry sauce, gravy and turkey, if desired.

chef tip:

This waffle may take longer to cook because of the stuffing and chicken stock.

CURRY WAFFLES

9-11 waffles • 10 minutes

A taste of India in a mini waffle! Curry spices and ginger combine for a waffle that's delicious on its own or ready for dipping in a classic Indian dish like chicken tikka masala or saag paneer.

Ingredients

1 ½ cups chickpea flour

¼ cup shredded cheddar cheese

1 tsp baking powder

¾ cup whole milk

2 large eggs

¼ cup ghee

2 tsp curry powder

¼ tsp ginger powder

Directions

1. Mix together chickpea flour, shredded cheddar, curry powder, ginger powder and baking powder in a large bowl.

2. Whisk together eggs, milk and ghee in a separate bowl. Add the wet ingredients to the dry and mix until just incorporated.

3. Add 3.5 tbsp of batter to your Mini Waffle Maker and cook until dark brown on both sides.

SCALLION WAFFLES

9-11 waffles · 20 minutes

Crunchy scallions and sesame seeds make this a perfect lunch or dinner treat!

Ingredients

1 cup finely chopped scallions

⅓ cup toasted sesame seeds

4 cloves minced garlic

1 large egg

¼ cup vegetable oil

¾ cup whole milk

1 tsp sesame oil

½ tsp salt

¼ tsp sugar

1 cup all-purpose flour

½ tbsp baking powder

⅛ tsp five-spice powder

⅛ tsp Sichuan pepper powder

⅛ tsp fresh ground white pepper

Directions

1. Toast the sesame seeds in a pan and cool completely.

2. Whisk together egg and oil until well-combined. Mix in whole milk, sesame oil, salt, sugar, flour, baking powder, five-spice powder, Sichuan peppercorn powder and fresh ground white pepper until well-combined.

3. Add scallions, garlic and toasted sesame seeds to the batter and mix until distributed evenly. Let the batter sit for 5 minutes.

4. Add 3.5 tbsp of batter to your Mini Waffle Maker and cook until golden brown on both sides.

MOROCCAN SPICE WAFFLE

6-8 waffles · 10 minutes

Inspired by the mystique of Marrakech and the warm flavors of Moroccan cuisine, these waffles are perfect when served with a side of hummus or a yogurt spread called labneh and a drizzle of olive oil.

Ingredients

1 tbsp Za'atar spice

1 tsp Harissa paste

⅓ cup whole wheat flour

⅔ cup all-purpose flour

2 tbsp baking powder

4 tbsp melted unsalted butter

1 large egg

½ cup whole milk

½ cup seltzer or club soda

Toppings

Hummus

Olive oil

chef tip:

If you can't find Za'atar spice, use 1 tbsp of thyme, marjoram, oregano & sesame seeds.

Directions

1. Mix together whole wheat flour, all-purpose flour and baking powder in a mixing bowl.

2. Whisk together milk, seltzer and egg in a separate bowl. While whisking, slowly drizzle the melted butter into the mix.

3. Add the wet ingredients to the dry ingredients and whisk until no clumps remain. Do not overmix the batter.

4. Mix in Za'atar spice and Harissa paste, whisking until the spices are all evenly distributed through the batter.

5. Add 3.5 tbsp of batter to your Mini Waffle Maker and cook until golden brown on both sides. Cut into wedges and serve with hummus and a drizzle of olive oil, if desired.

CRUNCHY CHEDDAR WAFFLES

6-8 waffles · 10 minutes

This waffle's cheesy Goldfish® crackers add the perfect crisp. Make them on their own, or pair them with your favorite soup for a lunchtime treat!

Ingredients

¾ cup pulverized Goldfish® crackers, cheddar flavor

¼ cup white sugar

½ tsp baking powder

1 large egg

1 ½ tbsp canola oil

1 cup whole milk

Directions

1. Mix together pulverized Goldfish®, sugar and baking powder.

2. Whisk together egg, oil and milk until smooth. Add in dry ingredients and mix until no clumps remain.

3. Add 3.5 tbsp of waffle mix to Mini Waffle Maker and cook until golden brown on both sides. Serve with maple syrup, if desired.

chef tip:

The waffle is crispiest when the Goldfish® bits are close to the outside edge.

ZUCCHINI PARMESAN WAFFLES 🥜

10-12 waffles · 20 minutes

Two classic Italian flavors make a savory snack that will have you craving seconds!

Ingredients

2 ½ cups shredded zucchini

1 large egg

¼ cups whole milk

2 tbsp flour

½ cups grated Parmigiano-Reggiano cheese

1 tbsp chopped parsley

2 pinches of salt

Pinch of pepper

Directions

1. Place shredded zucchini in a colander and toss with a pinch of salt.
   Let sit for 30 minutes.

2. Rinse well with cold water and squeeze out excess water. Dry on paper towels.

3. Whisk together egg, milk, Parmigiano and chopped parsley in a medium bowl.

4. In a separate bowl, combine flour, a pinch of salt and a pinch of pepper.

5. Add the seasoned flour mixture to the egg mixture. Fold in the zucchini.

6. Add 3.5 tbsp of batter to your Mini Waffle Maker and spread evenly. Cook to desired level of crisp.

FALAFEL WAFFLES

7-9 waffles · 25 minutes

Everyone loves a falafel waffle! The classic Mediterranean dish is transformed into crispy waffles that pair perfectly with cold cucumber salad and Tzatziki sauce.

Ingredients

¼ cup canned chickpeas, well rinsed

1 garlic clove

½ cup red onion, roughly chopped

1 handful fresh parsley leaves

1 cup baby spinach

1 tsp ground cumin

1 tsp ground coriander

1 tsp kosher or sea salt

Black pepper to taste

¼ cup extra virgin olive oil

½ cup chickpea flour

Oil for brushing

Directions

1. Mince garlic clove and onion.

2. Blend together all ingredients except the chickpea flour until well-combined.

3. Mix in chickpea flour after blending other ingredients.

4. Add 3.5 tbsp of batter to your Mini Waffle Maker and cook until golden brown on both sides.

BACON & CHEESE WAFFLES

8-10 waffles · 20 minutes

With crispy bacon bits dispersed throughout, this cheesy waffle marries sweet and savory worlds in one delectable breakfast combo.

Ingredients

1 cup all-purpose flour

2 tsp baking powder

1 large egg

1 cup whole milk

2 tbsp melted butter

½ cup grated cheese of choice

4 slices cooked bacon, crumbled

Directions

1. Whisk flour and baking powder together.

2. Whisk egg, milk, and butter together.

3. Fold wet ingredients into dry ingredients. Fold the grated cheese, and crumbled bacon into the waffle batter.

4. Add 3.5 tbsp of batter to your Mini Waffle Maker and cook until golden brown on both sides.

chef tip:

Prepare thick-cut bacon slabs for the best flavor.

CHEDDAR CORNBREAD WAFFLES

10-12 · 25 minutes

Dense, crumbly cornbread waffles made with buttermilk are a perfect complement to all your barbecue favorites. Serve with chili, pulled pork, and your favorite cole slaw for a perfect southern-style meal.

Ingredients

1 ½ cups all-purpose flour

1 cup yellow cornmeal

2 ½ tbsp sugar

2 tsp baking powder

1 tsp baking soda

2 cups buttermilk

2 large eggs

6 tbsp melted unsalted butter

2 ½ cups cheddar cheese

3 tbsp salt

Optional Toppings:

Shredded chicken or pork

Chili or vegetarian chili

Sour cream

Cilantro

Extra cheddar

Scallions

Directions

1. In a small pan over low heat melt butter. Shut off heat so butter is not hot when added to the mix.

2. Whisk together flour, cornmeal, baking powder and baking soda.

3. In a small bowl, whisk together the eggs, butter and buttermilk. Add the wet ingredients into the dry. Fold together until well-combined.

4. Mix in cheese.

5. Add 3.5 tbsp of batter to your Mini Waffle Maker and cook until golden brown on both sides.

GETTING CREATIVE

Hack that Mini Waffle Maker and try your hand at omelettes, s'mores, mac & cheese and more. Just because you haven't thought of it doesn't mean you can't conquer it!

CONFETTI WAFFLE CAKE

1 cake • 25 minutes

Inspired by Milk Bar in New York, this five-layer funfetti waffle cake is the easiest way to get the party started. The combo of fun rainbow sprinkles and vanilla frosting makes this a perfect treat for birthdays and other celebrations.

Ingredients

1 cup all-purpose flour

1 tbsp white sugar

2 tsp baking powder

¼ tsp salt

1 large egg

1 cup milk

2 tbsp melted unsalted butter

1 tsp real vanilla extract

1 ½ tbsp rainbow sprinkles

Vanilla Buttercream Frosting

3 cups confectioners sugar

¾ cup unsalted butter

1 tsp vanilla extract

1 tbsp heavy cream

chef tip:

To take the vanilla flavor over the top, we substitute vanilla bean paste!

Directions

1. Mix together flour, sugar, baking powder and salt in a medium bowl.

2. Whisk together milk, egg and melted butter and vanilla in a separate bowl. Add the wet ingredients to the dry and mix until combined. Add the rainbow sprinkles and mix to combine.

3. Add 3.5 tbsp of batter to your Mini Waffle Maker and cook until golden brown on both sides. Make five confetti waffles and allow a few minutes to cool.

4. For the frosting, mix confectioners sugar and butter together until smooth. Add vanilla extract and heavy cream. Spread frosting between each layer of "cake" with a spatula.

5. Top with a final layer of frosting and smooth the top. Finish with sprinkles.

MAC & CHEESE WAFFLES

10-12 waffles · 20 minutes

Everyone loves mac & cheese, so we wondered, will it waffle? The answer gave us this cheesy, delicious snack. Add your favorite mac & cheese fixings, like bacon or hot sauce, for an extra punch!

Ingredients

1 large egg

2 tbsp whole milk

1 cup cooked elbow macaroni

¼ cup Parmigiano-Reggiano cheese, grated

½ cup sharp cheddar cheese, shredded

¼ cup plain bread crumbs

½ tsp kosher salt

¼ tsp granulated garlic

¼ tsp onion powder

¼ tsp ground black pepper

¼ tsp white sugar

Directions

1. Whisk together egg and milk until smooth.

2. Mix together elbow macaroni, Parmigiano-Reggiano, cheddar, bread crumbs, salt, garlic, onion powder, pepper and sugar until combined. Add egg mixture and continue to stir until mixture reaches a sticky consistency.

3. Add 3 tbsp of batter to your Mini Waffle Maker. Cook until cheese has melted and crisped to golden brown on both sides.

CEREAL WAFFLES

8-10 waffles · 10 minutes

For lovers of breakfast cereal and cold milk, the cereal waffle is an enticing treat. It's a rare combination of sweetness, fluff and crunch in every bite.

Ingredients

½ cup crushed Corn Flakes®

¼ cup all-purpose flour

3 tbsp white sugar

½ tsp baking powder

1 large egg

1 tbsp canola oil

½ cup whole milk

¼ cup second cereal of your choice

Directions

1. Whisk together crushed Corn Flakes®, flour, sugar and baking powder.

2. Whisk together egg, oil and milk until smooth. Add in dry ingredients and mix until no clumps remain. Fold in second cereal.

3. Add 3 tbsp of batter to your Mini Waffle Maker and cook until golden brown on both sides.

S'MORES WAFFLES

8-10 waffles • 6 minutes

A traditional campfire treat perfected in your own Mini Waffle Maker. Bring the taste of the outdoors to your kitchen all year round!

Ingredients

¾ cup graham cracker crumbs

2 tbsp white sugar

½ tsp baking powder

1 large egg

⅖ cup whole milk

2 tbsp mini chocolate chips

¼ cup mini marshmallows

Directions

1. Mix together graham cracker crumbs, sugar and baking powder.

2. Whisk together egg and milk until smooth. Add in dry ingredients and mix until no clumps remain. Fold in chocolate chips and marshmallows.

3. Add 3 tbsp of batter to your Mini Waffle Maker and cook until golden brown on both sides. Serve with torched marshmallows and chocolate syrup, if desired.

GLAZED CHOCOLATE WAFFLE "DONUTS"

8-10 waffles · 10 minutes

Bringing together the best elements of a double-chocolate donut, these waffle "donuts" have a dense, moist interior and a sweet chocolate glaze.

Ingredients

1 cup all-purpose flour

¼ cup cocoa

½ tsp baking soda

¼ tsp salt

½ cup sugar

½ cup buttermilk

1 large egg

¼ cup oil

Chocolate Glaze

½ cup dark chocolate chips

2 tbsp unsalted butter

1 tbsp honey

2 tsp hot water

Directions for Donuts

1. Mix together flour, cocoa, baking soda, salt and sugar.

2. Whisk together buttermilk, egg, and oil. Add wet ingredients to dry ingredients and whisk until combined.

3. Add 3 tbsp of batter to your Mini Waffle Maker and cook until golden brown on both sides.

Directions for Chocolate Glaze

1. Melt chocolate chips in a double boiler over medium heat. Stir in butter and honey until completely melted.

2. Stir in hot water until glaze is thick and smooth.

chef tip:

To save time, melt chocolate in the microwave, pausing to stir every 15 seconds.

WAFFLE NUTMEG "DONUTS"

8-10 waffles • cook time

Nutmeg and creamy buttermilk come together for an autumn-inspired treat that's reminiscent of apple-cider donuts from the farmer's market.

Ingredients

1 cup all-purpose flour

⅓ cup sugar

1 tsp baking powder

¼ tsp nutmeg

¼ tsp salt

⅓ cup buttermilk

1 large egg

1 tablespoon melted unsalted butter

⅓ cup cinnamon sugar

Directions

1. Mix together flour, sugar, baking powder, nutmeg and salt.

2. Whisk together buttermilk, egg and butter.

3. Add 3 tbsp of batter to your Mini Waffle Maker and cook until golden brown on both sides. Dust with cinnamon sugar.

CHOCOLATE TACO WAFFLES

7-9 waffles · 10 minutes

What happens when you combine 3 all-star foods into one amazing treat? You'll just have to try filling these waffle-inspired taco shells with classic sundae ingredients to find out...

Ingredients

2 tbsp cocoa powder

½ cup all-purpose flour

⅔ cup white sugar

1 large egg

2 tbsp canola oil

½ cup whole milk

Directions

1. Mix together cocoa powder, flour and sugar.

2. Whisk together egg, oil and milk until smooth. Add dry ingredients and mix until no clumps remain.

3. Add 3 tbsp of batter to your Mini Waffle Maker and cook until crispy on both sides.

4. Remove waffles and immediately drape over a rolling pin, or similarly sized cylindrical object, to form taco shape. Let waffles cool on rolling pin for 3 minutes, then place in freezer.

5. Serve with ice cream, sprinkles and a caramel drizzle.

chef tip:

Add sprinkles to the batter for a sweet shell!

WAFFLED PINEAPPLE

with coconut cream

4 waffled pinapple slices • 6 minutes

A sweet, juicy pineapple slice toasted in your Mini Waffle Maker. Dusted in brown sugar and served with coconut cream, these deliciously sweet pineapple slices are a tropical treat that's gluten-free!

Ingredients

4 pineapple slices (circles)

2 teaspoons brown sugar

Toppings

Coconut cream

Directions

1. Sprinkle brown sugar onto pineapple rounds.

2. Place one pineapple round on your Mini Waffle Maker. Cook until hot with noticeable waffle pattern. Serve with coconut cream, if desired.

3. Repeat with other pineapple slices.

WAFFLE CHEESE FRITTERS

8-10 fritters • 6 minutes

With a tangy kick of hot sauce and two-cheese blend, these cheese fritters are anything but boring. Perfect for preparing ahead of time and saving as a snack!

Ingredients

1 cup shredded cheddar cheese

1 cup shredded Parmigiano-Reggiano cheese

1 tbsp all-purpose flour

1 tsp hot sauce

Directions

1. Mix cheeses with all-purpose flour. Add hot sauce and toss well.

2. Place 3 tbsp of mixture into the Dash Mini Waffle Maker and cook until crispy.

chef tip:

Add another splash of hot sauce if you're looking for more kick!

THE CHAFFLE

6 chaffles · 10 minutes

Start the morning off with a protein-rich snack! These chaffles keep well and are portable, so try making them all at the beginning of the week and freezing them to take on the go.

Ingredients

3 large eggs, beaten

½ onion, diced

½ pepper, diced

6 oz ham

1 cup Swiss cheese, grated

Directions

1. Whisk together beaten eggs, diced onion, diced pepper and grated Swiss cheese.

2. Pour 3 tbsp of the egg mixture into your Mini Waffle Maker. Add 2 oz of diced ham and cook for approximately 5 minutes.

MASHED POTATO BITE WAFFLES

4-6 waffles · 20 minutes

Mashed potatoes are one of our fave comfort foods, so why not waffle them? These mouth-watering patties are a great snack or side dish and pair well with sour cream or applesauce.

Ingredients

2 medium potatoes, peeled and cubed

1 tbsp unsalted butter

½ cup milk

1 tsp salt

Directions

1. Boil salted water on a stovetop. Peel and cube potatoes and add to water, cooking until tender but still firm.

2. Heat butter and milk in a pan over low heat until butter has melted. While mashing potatoes, slowly add milk mixture and salt to the pan until smooth and creamy.

3. Add 3 tbsp of mashed potatoes to your Mini Waffle Maker and cook until crispy.

CHOCOLATE CHIP COOKIE WAFFLE SUNDAE

8-10 cookies · 10 minutes

Make waffles a dessert centerpiece with a delicious waffle sundae on a cookie base. Creating and personalizing your own sundae is fun for the whole family!

Ingredients

1 cup all-purpose flour

½ tsp baking soda

½ cup softened unsalted butter

⅜ cup brown sugar

2 tbsp white sugar

1 large egg

½ tsp vanilla extract

1 cup mini chocolate chips

Toppings

Ice cream

Chocolate syrup

Whipped cream

Walnuts

Cherry

Sprinkles

Directions

1. Whisk together flour, baking soda, butter, egg, sugar and vanilla extract in a large bowl. Pour in chocolate chips and stir until combined.

2. Add 2.5 tbsp of the cookie dough to your Mini Waffle Maker and cook until golden brown on both sides. Serve with desired toppings.

WAFFLED CINNAMON ROLL

5 rolls • 5 minutes

Did you know you can make a cinnamon roll in your Mini Waffle Maker? For a warm, cinnamon-y treat, we give you a crispy delectable cinnamon roll, waffle-ized!

Ingredients

7 oz cinnamon roll dough (or 1 tube), with icing

Toppings

Icing

Powdered sugar

Cinnamon sugar

Directions

1. Place 1 cinnamon roll in your Mini Waffle Maker.

2. Cook for 2-3 minutes, or until golden brown.

3. Serve with the reserved icing from your tube of cinnamon roll dough. Enjoy!

chef tip:

You can freeze individual cinnamon rolls and then make them one at a time.

FRENCH TOAST WAFFLE

6-8 waffles · 10 minutes

In France, French toast is known as "Pain Perdu" because it's made with "Lost" day-old baguette. Dry bread soaks up batter better than fresh bread, so the only thing lost is our will to stop at just one slice.

Ingredients

4 stale slices of white bread or baguette, 1 ½" thick

3 tbsp sugar

2 large eggs

1 cup whole milk

¼ tsp vanilla extract

½ tsp cinnamon

Melted butter for basting the Mini Waffle Maker

Directions

1. If using white bread, use a 5" circle cutter to cut the bread into rounds. Thick bread works best for this recipe.

2. Whisk together milk, eggs, cinnamon, sugar and vanilla extract in a medium bowl. Dip bread into the mixture until fully saturated.

3. Baste Mini Waffle Maker with butter and cook soaked bread till golden brown.

chef tip:

No stale bread? Leave a few slices out overnight or very lightly toast the bread.

WAFFLED APPLE PIE

2 mini pies · 6 minutes

This easy recipe will have you making flaky, buttery waffle pies in no time. Top with a scoop of ice cream and caramel drizzle for all-American goodness.

Ingredients

2 circular 4" pie crusts

3 tbsp chunky applesauce

Pinch of cinnamon

Pinch of nutmeg

Toppings

Ice cream scoop

Caramel drizzle

Directions

1. Lay pie crust flat on the bottom of your Mini Waffle Maker and top with 3 tbsp of chunky applesauce. Add pinches of cinnamon and nutmeg. Cook until applesauce mixture is warm.

2. Top with ice cream and caramel drizzle, if desired.

chef tip:

Close the lid gently to avoid breaking the pie crust.

WAFFLES BENEDICT

6-8 waffles · 25 minutes

Bring your brunch game to the next level. This recipe makes a restaurant-style breakfast out of the Classic Waffle, topped with poached eggs and a homemade hollandaise sauce.

Ingredients

1 cup all-purpose flour

1 tbsp sugar

2 tsp baking powder

¼ tsp salt

1 large egg

1 cup milk

2 tbsp softened unsalted butter

For Eggs Benedict

2 large eggs

½ bunch asparagus, trimmed and boiled

4 strips Canadian-style bacon

2 tbsp softened unsalted butter

Chives or cayenne pepper

For Hollandaise Sauce

4 large egg yolks

3 ½ tbsp lemon juice

1 tbsp water

1 cup melted unsalted butter

Pinch of salt

Pinch of white pepper

chef tip:

Add the egg yolk mixture to the hollandaise sauce 1 tbsp at a time to avoid ruining consistency.

Directions

1. Mix together flour, sugar, baking powder and salt in a medium bowl.

2. Whisk together milk, egg and melted butter in a separate bowl. Add the wet ingredients to the dry and mix until combined.

3. Add 3.5 tbsp of batter to your Mini Waffle Maker and cook until golden brown on both sides.

4. To make the Hollandaise sauce, fill the bottom of a double boiler part-way with water. Make sure that water does not touch the bottom of the bowl. Bring water to a gentle simmer on the stovetop.

5. In the top of the double boiler, whisk together egg yolks, lemon juice, white pepper, and 1 tbsp water.

6. Slowly add melted butter to the egg yolk mixture while whisking. If the sauce becomes too thick, add a splash of water.

7. Add salt and continue whisking until fully incorporated. Remove from heat and cover with a lid to keep the sauce warm.

For assembling your Eggs Benedict

Top a prepared waffle with one poached egg, bacon, and cooked asparagus. Drizzle with hollandaise sauce. Garnish with chives or cayenne pepper.

BUTTERMILK FRIED CHICKEN & WAFFLES

9-11 waffles • 30 minutes

An absolutely essential southern classic, buttermilk fried chicken sits on a throne of mini waffles. The crispy fried coating tastes best when doused in maple syrup or honey.

Ingredients

1 cup all-purpose flour

1 tbsp sugar

1 tsp baking powder

½ tsp baking soda

1 cup buttermilk

2 tbsp melted unsalted butter

1 tsp vanilla extract

1 large egg

½ tsp salt

For Buttermilk Fried Chicken

1 lb boneless chicken breasts, sliced

½ cup and 3 tbsp buttermilk, divided

¾ cup all-purpose flour

½ tsp black pepper

½ tsp garlic powder

½ tsp paprika

1 tsp baking powder

2 cups vegetable oil

1 tsp salt

chef tip:

Be careful when placing chicken tenders in the hot oil. Use tongs to gently add them one at a time.

continued on next page →

Buttermilk Fried Chicken & Waffles continued...

Directions

1. Mix together flour, sugar, baking powder, baking soda and salt in a medium bowl.

2. Whisk egg, buttermilk, vanilla and melted butter together in a separate bowl. Add wet ingredients to the dry and mix until combined.

3. Add 3.5 tbsp of batter to your Mini Waffle Maker and cook until golden brown on both sides.

For Buttermilk Fried Chicken

1. Slice chicken breast into tenders.

2. Prepare the breading by mixing together the flour, salt, pepper, garlic powder, paprika and baking powder in a small dish. Stir in 3 tbsp of buttermilk. Pour ½ cup of buttermilk in a separate medium dish.

3. Dip the chicken tenders first in the buttermilk and then in the breading. Place on a baking sheet lined with aluminum foil.

4. Pour ¾ of the vegetable oil in a high-sided pot and heat on high until the oil simmers. Use tongs to place chicken tenders in the oil. Cook until golden brown, then flip to cook the other side. Remove chicken tenders from oil and place on a paper towel-lined plate to dry.

5. Once dry, place chicken on top of waffles and drizzle with maple syrup.

EGG & CHEESE HASH BROWN WAFFLES

8-10 waffles · 20 minutes

Stuffed with breakfast favorites, these waffles cut out the griddle or skillet to make a cheesy potato hash brown right in your Mini Waffle Maker!

Ingredients

2 ½ cups frozen shredded hash brown potatoes

2 large eggs

¼ cup whole milk

1 ½ cups shredded cheddar cheese

¼ cup chopped chives

Pinch of salt

Pinch of pepper

Directions

1. Lay out frozen hash browns on a cookie sheet lined with paper towels for at least 15 minutes. While potatoes thaw, gather the rest of the ingredients.

2. Whisk together eggs and milk in a medium bowl.

3. Mix in potatoes, cheese and chives. Season with salt and pepper.

4. Add 3.5 tbsp of batter to your Mini Waffle Maker and cook until golden brown on both sides.

SUNDAY MORNING BAGEL WAFFLE

8-10 waffles •10 minutes

Bagels or waffles? Why not both! These delicious "bagels" are perfect for spreading with your favorite schmear and topping with some smoked salmon.

Ingredients

⅓ cup whole wheat flour

⅔ cup all-purpose flour

2 tbsp baking powder

4 tbsp melted unsalted butter

1 large egg

⅓ cup everything bagel spice

½ cup milk

½ cup seltzer or club soda

Directions

1. Mix together whole wheat flour, all-purpose flour and baking powder in a mixing bowl with ¼ cup everything bagel spice.

2. Whisk together milk, seltzer and egg in a separate bowl. While whisking, slowly drizzle melted butter into the mix.

3. Add wet ingredients to the dry ingredients and whisk until no clumps remain. Do not overmix the batter.

4. Add 3.5 tbsp of batter to your Mini Waffle Maker. Sprinkle remaining everything bagel spice on top and shut the lid. Cook until surface is firm on both sides.

chef tip:

Make a "bagel" with scallion cream cheese, lox and a slice of red onion.

WAFFLE POPS

10-12 waffle pops · 15 minutes

Double down with waffle pops! This recipe combines every baker's two loves: baking and decorating. Get creative with marshmallows, chocolate, sprinkles and more for a kid-friendly treat that everyone can love.

Ingredients

1 cup all-purpose flour

1 tbsp sugar

2 tsp baking powder

¼ tsp salt

1 large egg

1 cup milk

2 tbsp softened unsalted butter

For Waffle Pop Coating

1 cup vanilla frosting

¾ cup cereal of your choice

½ cup rainbow sprinkles

¼ cup water

Toppings

Chocolate sauce

Mini marshmallows

chef tip:

Make sure the popsicle sticks are sturdily inside each waffle to avoid slippage when coating.

continued on next page ⟶

Waffle Pops continued...

Directions

1. Mix together flour, sugar, baking powder and salt in a medium bowl.

2. Whisk together milk, egg and melted butter in a separate bowl. Add the wet ingredients to the dry and mix until just incorporated.

3. Add 2 tbsp of batter to your Mini Waffle Maker and cook until golden brown on both sides.

4. Vertically insert popsicle stick through each waffle while warm.

For Waffle Pop Coating

1. Mix together frosting, cereal, water and sprinkles in a medium bowl.

2. Once each waffle is attached to a popsicle stick, hold the edge of each stick furthest from the waffle and dip waffle into coating bowl.

3. Use the popsicle stick to twirl each waffle while pulling away from the coating mixture bowl.

4. Top with chocolate sauce drizzle and mini marshmallows, if desired.

WAFFLE SAMMIES

This assortment of pizzas, quesadillas, ice cream sandwiches and more has redefined the idea of a sandwich. You'll be falling in love with sandwich-style waffles in no time!

VANILLA WAFFLE
ICE CREAM SAMMIES

4 sammies · 15 minutes

On a hot summer day, you can't go wrong with an ice cream sandwich! Create your own with two mini waffles and a scoop of your favorite ice cream. Dip in chocolate or roll in sprinkles for added flair.

Ingredients

1 ½ cups all-purpose flour

1 tsp baking powder

1 cup white sugar

2 large eggs

1 tbsp unsalted butter

¾ tsp vanilla extract

1 cup whole milk

Ice Cream Sandwich

2 scoops of ice cream

¼ cup melted chocolate chips

2 tsp sprinkles

Directions

1. Whisk together flour, baking powder and sugar.

2. Whisk together eggs, butter, vanilla extract and milk until smooth. Add in dry ingredients and mix until no clumps remain.

3. Add 3.5 tbsp of batter to your Mini Waffle Maker and cook until golden brown on both sides.

4. Place finished waffles on parchment paper lined sheet trays and freeze for one hour.

5. Place 2 scoops of ice cream on top of one frozen waffle. Use a level surface to flatten the tops of the ice cream scoops.

6. Add another frozen waffle and squeeze gently.

7. Dip sandwich in melted chocolate and roll in sprinkles, if desired.

chef tip:

Cook a little longer than usual for a crispier and firmer ice cream sammie.

BLT WAFFLE SAMMIES

3 sammies · 15 minutes

Our take on a deli favorite, this BLT uses waffles instead of bread. The nooks & crannies of the waffle are perfect for spreading with mayo or your condiment of choice!

Ingredients

6 Happy Medium Whole Wheat Waffles

6 slices of bacon

½ head of lettuce, sliced

1 tomato, sliced

2 tbsp mayonnaise

Directions

1. Prepare waffles as instructed in Happy Medium Whole Wheat Waffles on page 18.

2. Lay one prepared waffle flat. Spread a layer of mayo.

3. Top with bacon, lettuce, tomato. Complete with your second waffle.

SWEET POTATO EGG SAMMIES

4 sammies · 15 minutes

With sweet potato waffles serving as the bookends of this bacon and egg sandwich, everything you could ever want in a breakfast can be on one plate.

Ingredients

¾ cups sweet potato purée

1 ½ tbsp canola oil

½ cup whole milk

1 large egg

½ cup all-purpose flour

½ tsp baking powder

¼ cup light brown sugar

1 tsp salt

For Egg & Bacon Sandwich:

2 large eggs

3 tbsp whole milk

¼ tsp kosher salt

Pinch of ground black pepper

2 tsp canola oil

2 slices bacon

2 tsp honey (optional)

Directions

1. Mix together sweet potato purée, oil, milk and egg until smooth.

2. Whisk together flour, baking powder, brown sugar and salt. Add to wet ingredients and mix until no clumps remain.

3. Add 3.5 tbsp of batter to your Mini Waffle Maker and cook until golden brown on both sides.

For Egg & Bacon Sandwich:

1. Preheat oven to 400°F.

2. Whisk together eggs, milk, salt and pepper until smooth. Heat oil in a small fry pan over medium heat until slick and shiny.

3. Add eggs and reduce heat to low. Scramble eggs while stirring continuously.

4. Place bacon on resting rack over sheet tray and bake until satisfactory.

5. Lay one prepared waffle flat. Top with scrambled eggs, bacon, and a drizzle of honey. Complete with your second waffle.

WAFFLE CLUB SAMMIES 🥜

2 sammies • 10 minutes

This wafflized version of a brunch classic highlights the seasoned turkey, while the mayo flavorfully binds the ingredients to the fluffy waffles.

Ingredients

6 Happy Medium Whole Wheat Waffles

¼ cup mayonnaise

6 slices of bacon

1 tomato, sliced

¼ cup basil

6 leaves of lettuce

½ lb sliced turkey breast

Pinch of salt

Pinch of ground pepper

Directions

1.   Prepare waffles as instructed in Happy Medium Whole Wheat Waffles on page 18.

2.   Lay one prepared waffle flat. Spread a thin layer of mayo, then top with some turkey, lettuce, basil, 1 strip of bacon, tomato, salt and pepper. Top with a second waffle. Repeat the ingredient pattern.

3.   Complete your club sandwich with a third waffle and seal the club with a toothpick.

AVOCADO "TOAST" WAFFLES

7-9 waffles • 7 minutes

This recipe is a great power snack. It uses our Happy Medium Whole Wheat Waffle recipe as a bed for the omega-3 rich avocado euphoria.

Ingredients

⅓ cup whole wheat flour

⅔ cup all-purpose flour

2 tbsp baking powder

4 tbsp melted unsalted butter

1 large egg

½ cup milk

½ cup seltzer or club soda

Avocado Topping

2 ripe avocados

Pinch of crushed red pepper flakes

Pinch of sea salt

2 tbsp extra virgin olive oil for drizzling

Directions

1. Mix together whole wheat flour, all-purpose flour and baking powder in a mixing bowl.

chef tip:

Add a fried egg on top for some added protein and savory treat.

continued on next page ⟶

Avocado "Toast" Waffles continued...

2. Mix together milk, seltzer and egg in a separate bowl. While mixing, slowly drizzle the melted butter into the bowl. Add the wet ingredients to the dry ingredients and whisk until no clumps remain.

3. Add 3.5 tbsp of batter to your Mini Waffle Maker and cook until golden brown on both sides.

4. While the mini waffle is cooking, slice avocado lengthwise and remove the pit. Scoop the meat into a mixing bowl and mash with a fork until smooth.

5. Once the waffle is cooked, spread the mashed avocado on the waffle and drizzle with olive oil. Sprinkle crushed red pepper flakes and sea salt over the top, if desired.

WAFFLE QUESADILLAS

4 waffle quesadillas • 20 minutes

This recipe brings all the features of a southwest fave to the realm of waffles. With beans, corn, shredded chicken, guacamole and more, this waffle quesadilla is a snack that's sure to satisfy.

Ingredients

8 Happy Medium Whole Wheat Waffles

2 ½ cup shredded cheddar

1 cup black beans

1 cup corn

1 sliced avocado

Toppings

Shredded chicken breast

Sour cream

Pico de gallo

Guacamole

Salsa

Directions

1. Prepare waffles as instructed in Happy Medium Whole Wheat Waffles on page 16.

2. Mix together beans, cheese, avocado and corn in a medium bowl.

3. Lay one prepared waffle flat. Top with 2.5 tbsp of beans, cheese, avocado, and corn mixture. Complete with your second waffle and press together until the cheese becomes melty.

4. Add desired toppings.

chef tip:

Cook waffles slightly longer for a crunchier bite!

GRILLED CHEESE SAMMIES

3 sammies • 5 minutes

Perfect for kids, this simple sandwich is a great lunch or snack. With buttery waffles and melty cheese sauce, it's a comfort-food that everyone can love.

Ingredients

6 Happy Medium Whole Wheat Waffles

1 cup shredded cheddar cheese

1 cup shredded Monterey Jack cheese

Directions

1. Prepare waffles as instructed in Happy Medium Whole Wheat Waffles on page 18.

2. Mix cheeses and melt mixture. Top one waffle with 3 tbsp of cheese mixture and press another waffle on top until cheese oozes.

FANCY GRILLED CHEESE SAMMIES

3 sammies • 7 minutes

If you want to take fromage-on-bread to the next level, this is the recipe for you. Upgrade to triple-cream brie and sweet raspberry jam, and you'll be feasting on a delicious, luxurious snack in no time. Pinkies up!

Ingredients

6 Happy Medium Whole Wheat Waffles

3 slices brie cheese

½ cup raspberry jam

Directions

1. Prepare waffles as instructed in Happy Medium Whole Wheat Waffles on page 18.

2. Lay one waffle flat and top with 1 slice of cheese and spread jam on top. Lay another waffle on top and press together until cheese and jam begin to ooze.

Also try these cheeses:

Camambert

Havarti

Swiss

Asiago

Goat cheese

Feta

WAFFLE BISCUIT PIZZA

8-10 pizzas • 8 minutes

With all your favorite pizza toppings sealed inside one waffle, this recipe packs everything you love about pizza into a biscuit.

Ingredients

1 cup all-purpose flour

½ tbsp baking powder

6 tbsp milk

¼ tsp salt

¼ cup cold unsalted butter

½ cup shredded mozzarella cheese

Preferred fillings (pepperoni, onions, peppers, sausage, etc.)

Directions

1. Whisk together flour, baking powder and salt.

2. Add the butter and use a pastry cutter or fork to cut butter into flour until coarse. Stir in milk.

3. Roll dough out on a floured surface until roughly 0.5" thick. Cut out as many 3" circles as possible. Slice each dough circle in half (roughly 0.25" thick).

4. Cut dough circles horizontally. Stuff with mozzarella and other desired fillings. Once filled, seal the pouch by pinching the edges of the dough.

5. Add one pouch at a time to the Mini Waffle Maker until golden and crispy. Serve with a side of marinara sauce for dipping, if desired.

chef tip:

Use store-bought refrigerated biscuit dough as a shortcut!

INDEX

INDEX

INDEX

COPYRIGHT NOTICES

MINI IS MIGHTY!

Meet some of our other *mini makers...*

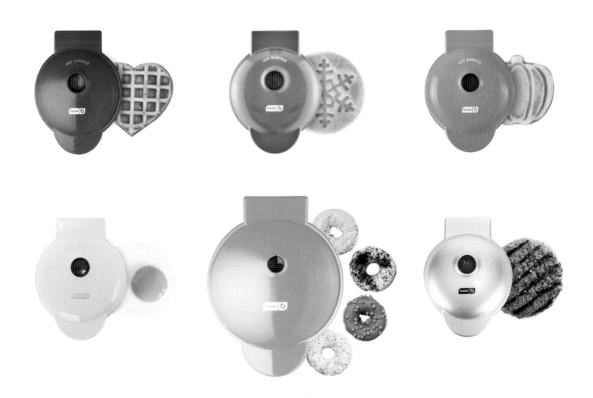

Want even more minis? **Check out bydash.com** for our latest & greatest additions.

GRATITUDE

A very special *thank you* to all the individuals who made this book possible and for their countless hours of Mini Waffle making!

EDITORIAL DIRECTOR: Catherine-Gail Reinhard
EXECUTIVE EDITOR: Daniel Dash
ASSOCIATE EDITOR: Colin Heasley
RECIPE DEVELOPMENT & TESTING: Adam C. Banks, Jenny Dorsey, Catherine-Gail Reinhard, Caitlin Wise, Anastasiia Vlasova
DESIGN DIRECTOR: Amy Silverman-Miller
STAFF PHOTOGRAPHER: Julian Master
ADDITIONAL PHOTOGRAPHY: Jenny Dorsey, Catherine-Gail Reinhard
FOOD STYLING: Adam C. Banks, Jenny Dorsey, Catherine-Gail Reinhard, Ansastasiia Vlasova
PRODUCTION COORDINATOR: Ansastasiia Vlasova
ILLUSTRATIONS: Joe Geis, Amy Silverman-Miller
FRONT & BACK COVER PHOTOGRAPHY: Julian Master
COVER DESIGN: Matthew Pisane & Amy Silverman-Miller

the DASH FAMILY

We believe that the path to health and wellness starts with cooking at home. From our headquarters in New York City, our team works tirelessly to develop tools that make it easier for you to prepare and enjoy home-cooked meals using natural, unprocessed ingredients. Our mission is to make healthy home cooking easier so that you can feel your best. That's what unprocessed living is all about!

Join the fam!  Follow us on instagram for recipes, videos, and daily inspiration @unprocessyourfood

THE WAFFLE CREW

Everyday we're wafflin'... At Dash, we've been busy dreaming up all kinds of delicious waffle recipes. From the kitchen to the studio, our crew has been measuring, cooking, sampling, styling, snapping, and designing this book to inspire you to broaden your waffle-making horizons. We hope that our recipes motivate you to grab a Mini Waffle Maker, get into the kitchen and make something delicious. Happy waffling!

CATHERINE REINHARD

Ringmaster

JENNY DORSEY

Recipe Guru

CAITLIN WISE

Ms. Dash

AMY SILVERMAN-MILLER

Design Ace

JULIAN MASTER

Photo Snapper

ANASTASIIA VLASOVA

Studio Wrangler

DANIEL DASH

Utility Player

COLIN HEASLEY

Copy Pro